Elephants

James Maclaine

Designed by Will Dawes

Illustrated by John Francis

Additional illustration by Tim Haggerty

Elephant consultant: Caitlin O'Connell-Rodwell, Ph.D., Instructor, Stanford University School of Medicine
Reading consultant: Alison Kelly, Principal Lecturer at Roehampton University

Contents

Jumbo giants

Elephants are the largest land animals.
They can live until they're 70 years old.

An adult male elephant can
weigh as much as 60 people.

African elephants

African elephants live in forests or on grassy plains called savannahs.

These are African savannah elephants. They are the largest type of elephant.

Two long curved teeth stick out of their mouths. They are called tusks.

4

African forest elephants live deep in thick, leafy rainforests.

They are smaller and have much straighter tusks than savannah elephants.

All elephants have wrinkly skin and huge ears. They flap their ears to cool down.

Asian elephants

Asian elephants are shorter and lighter than African elephants.

They have two bumps on the tops of their heads and have smaller ears than African elephants.

Many Asian elephants don't have tusks.

There are different types of
Asian elephants.

Indian and Sri Lankan elephants have pink
patches of skin on their bodies.

Borneo elephants
have very long tails.

Sumatran elephants
have pale skin.

Trunk tricks

Elephants have long, strong noses that they can bend. These are called trunks. Elephants use their trunks to drink.

An elephant dips the end of its trunk into water and sucks some up.

When its trunk is full of water, the elephant points it at its mouth.

Then, the elephant squirts the water out of its trunk and drinks it.

Elephants also smell, feel and grab things with their trunks.

This elephant is using its trunk to pick leaves to eat.

Tough tusks

Elephants have different ways of using their strong tusks.

They use them to rip tasty roots from the ground.

They also rest their heavy trunks on their tusks.

Male elephants use their tusks when they fight.

These elephants are digging in mud with their tusks, to find salt.

Elephants eat salt to stay healthy.

Elephant talk

Elephants show how they feel by what they do and the noises they make.

These elephants are saying hello to each other by touching their trunks.

When elephants are frightened, they lift up their tails.

When they are excited, they flap their ears quickly.

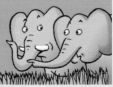

Angry elephants charge and make loud noises.

Elephants make very low sounds to each other that people can't hear.

Happy families

Elephants live in groups called herds.

This large herd is crossing a marsh.

It is made up of female elephants and their young.

The oldest and largest female usually takes care of the herd.

She leads the rest of the elephants when they're on the move.

When the weather is dry she knows where to find water.

She keeps watch while the herd rests in the shade.

She guides the others when they cross rivers.

Bull elephants

Male elephants are called bulls. When they are about twelve years old, bulls leave their herds.

Some bull elephants live on their own.

Others live together in small groups.

When bull elephants want to meet females, they visit a herd.

Sometimes bull elephants fight to find out who is the strongest.

These young bull elephants are pushing each other with their heads and tusks.

Big baby

A mother elephant carries her baby inside her for nearly two years. A baby elephant is called a calf.

This is an Asian elephant calf. Young calves have fuzzy hair on their heads.

When a calf is born, the other elephants come to greet it.

If it can't stand on its own, the mother helps it to get up.

Soon, the calf can walk. It stays close to its mother.

The calf drinks its mother's milk many times a day.

Elephant calves like to suck the ends of their trunks.

Growing up

As a calf grows up, it gets help from older elephants in the herd.

A calf finds shade by standing under a bigger elephant.

If a calf gets stuck in mud, the other elephants help to pull it out.

Members of the herd protect the calf from dangerous lions.

Step by step, calves
learn how to look
after themselves
by copying
older elephants.

This calf is learning how to pick
and eat grass.

Big eaters

Elephants spend a lot of time finding the food they like to eat.

They shake fruit and seeds down from trees.

They pluck clumps of grass with the tips of their trunks.

They strip away tree bark with their tusks and trunks.

This elephant is reaching up to pick leafy branches from a tree.

Elephants wear down their teeth by chewing, but they grow new ones.

At rest

Elephants only sleep for a few hours each night, but they take naps during the day.

Many elephants shut their eyes and sleep standing up.

Some lean against tree trunks while they rest.

Other elephants lie down and use bushes as pillows.

Some elephants snore when they are asleep.

This elephant calf is trying to rest, but the others want to play.

Splashing around

Elephants visit rivers and watering holes to wash, drink and play.

Elephants lie in water with the rest of their herd.

They also roll in mud baths to cool themselves down.

Then, they spray dust on their bodies to protect their skin from the sun.

Elephants are excellent swimmers.

This Asian elephant is swimming in the sea.

It is using its trunk like a snorkel to breathe underwater.

Saving elephants

Some people hunt elephants or destroy the places where they live. Other people are trying to save them.

These young elephants have lost their families. They will be looked after until they're old enough to return to the wild.

People care for the elephants and feed them bottles of milk several times a day.

Someone sleeps next to each elephant to keep it company at night.

As they grow up, the elephants gradually join herds living in the wild.

Years later, elephants still remember the people who cared for them.

Glossary

Here are some of the words in this book you might not know. This page tells you what they mean.

 savannah - a grassy area with very few trees and bushes.

 tusk - a long, curved tooth that sticks out of an elephant's mouth.

 trunk - an elephant's long and strong nose that it can bend.

 herd - a large or small group of elephants who live together.

 bull - a male elephant. Grown-up bulls live alone or in small groups.

 calf - a baby elephant. Most mother elephants have one calf at a time.

 watering hole - a pool of water where animals drink and bathe.

Websites to visit

You can visit exciting websites to find out more about elephants.

To visit these websites, go to the Usborne Quicklinks Website at **www.usborne-quicklinks.com** Read the internet safety guidelines, and then type the keywords "**beginners elephants**".

The websites are regularly reviewed and the links in Usborne Quicklinks are updated. However, Usborne Publishing is not responsible, and does not accept liability, for the content or availability of any website other than its own. We recommend that children are supervised while on the internet.

Elephants enjoy having a shower. They suck up water with their trunks and spray it over their bodies.

Index

Acknowledgements

Photographic manipulation by John Russell

Photo credits
The publishers are grateful to the following for permission to reproduce material:
cover © **Ferrero-Labat/ardea.com**; p1 © **Frans Lanting/FLPA**; p2-3 © **Martyn Colbeck/Oxford Scientific (OSF)/photolibrary.com**; p4-5 © **Anup Shah/naturepl.com**; p6 © **Kevin Schafer/Peter Arnold Images/photolibrary.com**; p9 © **Image100/photolibrary.com**; p11 © **Mark MacEwen/Oxford Scientific (OSF)/photolibrary.com**; p12-13 © **John Cancalosi/Peter Arnold Images/photolibrary.com**; p14 © **Robert Harding/Robert Harding Travel/photolibrary.com**; p17 © **Chris Johns/National Geographic/Getty Images**; p18 © **William Albert Allard/National Geographic Stock**; p21 © **Juergen & Christine Sohns/Picture Press/photolibrary.com**; p23 © **HEINRICH VAN DEN BERG/WWI/Still Pictures/photolibrary.com**; p25 © **Martin Harvey/Peter Arnold Images/photolibrary.com**; p27 © **Steve Bloom/stevebloom.com**; p28 © **Jon Hrusa/epa/Corbis**; p31 © **Martin Harvey/The Image Bank/Getty Images**

Every effort has been made to trace and acknowledge ownership of copyright. If any rights have been omitted, the publishers offer to rectify this in any subsequent editions following notification.

Sun, moon and stars

Farm animals

Elizabeth I

RUBBISH AND RECYCLING

Dogs

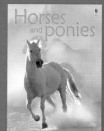
Horses and ponies

Spiders

Planes

Ancient Greeks

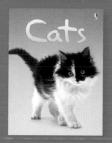
Cats

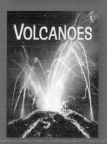
VOLCANOES

DINOSAURS

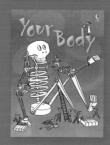
Your Body

Armour

Sharks

Celts

Vikings

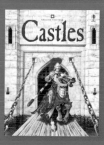
Castles

How flowers grow

Digging up the past

Living in space

Caterpillars and Butterflies

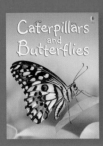
Ballet

Pirates

Egyptians

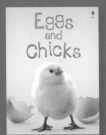
Eggs and Chicks

Romans

Weather

Tadpoles and frogs

Why do we eat?

Under the sea

Bears

Aztecs

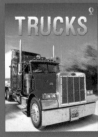
TRUCKS

Night Animals

Firefighters

Antarctica

Bugs

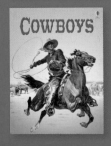
COWBOYS

Planet Earth